Fast Arrow Speaks

The Forgotten Ones

Diana Dörr

About the Author and Fast Arrow

Diana Dörr is an alternative practitioner and Trance Medium with many years of her own practice in Bad Homburg (Germany). In 2011 she published her first novel „Der Steg nach Tatarka" at Paracelsus Verlag in Salzburg/ Austria. In her books, the author combines her connection with nature with her professional interests, the healing of people and Mother Earth.

The book "Fast Arrow Speaks" was developed during her Home Circle in trance control. It repeats the messages of her spirit guides concerning the Covid-19 pandemic in 2020. The spokesman for this spirit guide group is the North American Indian "Fast Arrow", who is also the author's Spirit Control. He also works in trance control through the author in her healing practice and in her mediumship circles.

You can find out more about the author here:
https://www.dianadoerr.de/
https://www.dianadoerr-medium.de/

Other books by the author:

Der Steg nach Tatarka
Aurora in geheimer Mission
Erdheilung kinderleicht gemacht
Aurora und der Wächter des Wassers
Auroras Heilquellenführer

Fast Arrow Speaks

The Forgotten Ones

Diana Dörr

The information in this book dös not replace the diagnosis,
advice, examination and therapy of a doctor and should not lead
to discontinuing or changing previous therapies or medications.

»Fast Arrow Speaks - The Forgotten Ones«
© 2021 Diana Dörr

Author: Diana, Dörr
Cover Design: © Donna Dean

Publishing and print: tredition GmbH, Halenreie 42,
22359 Hamburg
ISBN 978-3-347-26509-7 (Paperback)
ISBN 978-3-347-26510-3 (Hardcover)
ISBN 978-3-347-26511-0 (e-Book)

Bibliographic information published by the Deutsche
Nationabibliothek:
The Deutsche Nationalbibliothek lists this publication in the
Deutsche Nationalbibliografie; detailed bibliographic data are
available on the internet: http://dnb.d-nb.de.

Contents

Introduction

My first contact with other worlds was during a near-death experience in a car accident more than 20 years ago. Since then I have realized that there is more than what we can perceive with our normal senses, and that life is not over with death. It was then that for the first time I was able to see my guardian angel, who brought me back to this Earth plane. I believe he is still part of my spirit guide team.

This was followed by more touching experiences with the spiritual world, which I recorded in my first book "Der Steg nach Tatarka".

During the time in which I wrote the novel „Der Steg nach Tatarka" and experienced what is described in it myself, I also had first experiences in automatic writing and further encounters with the spiritual world. But I did not trust myself and the spiritual world for a long time and did not know how to deal with these gifts.

In 2008, during a trip to Hawaii, I was unexpectedly told by a medium and Kahuna that I was also a full trance medium and had a job to do with this.

At this time, however, I did not understand what this meant, and how I could train and use this ability.

Without my being aware of it at the time, this ability first flowed into my shamanic work, my Earth healing books and Earth healing circles.

For many years I attended various advanced training courses for mediums from Germany, England and the USA in order not only to develop my medium skills, but also to understand them. The so-called mental mediumship to get in touch with the deceased I learned during this time was not what I was looking for and put too much pressure on me. Parallel to this training, I sat in closed and open development circles in silence for many years, at least one hour a week, often in two circles a week. This was my greatest apprenticeship and brought me to a point in my medium development where I became aware of what it meant to be a trance medium and what the word trance really meant. Trance mediumship cannot be learned in a weekend course, and trance control is hardly known in Germany. It has nothing to do with „channeling". During this development circle I knew intuitively that I would no longer get any further in my development alone, and that I needed good teachers for my development.

During the Covid-19 pandemic I used the quiet lockdown time to continue my education in trance control, and today I see it as a lucky coincidence for my medium path.

It was especially through Steven Upton, a teacher of The Spiritualists' National Union, that I became aware that I am a trance control medium and learned how to deepen this skill further. On his advice, I founded a Home Circle in autumn 2020 and found people who were willing to sit as sitters for me.

Many of the following messages and the healing energies that were transmitted were intended for these participants. But the messages affect far more people during this time as I quickly realized.

At the request of many of the participants in the Home Circle I have now put the messages of my spirit guides together on paper, as not so many participants were possible due to the Covid-19 pandemic distance rules, and I had to refuse many sitters. In this way I would like to make the messages of the spirits, who call themselves the "Forgotten Ones", accessible to even more people. May the words of the "Forgotten Ones" touch many hearts and help them get through these special times.

My spirit guides, teachers and philosophers certainly had a good reason to speak English in this Home Circle, so I have decided to leave these messages as they are and to publish the original in English.

As a result, the words of the „Forgotten Ones" can not only reach more people, but will also pass on the original vibration of the words, which feels very different from the translation. Nevertheless, I surely will translate the words of my spirit guides into German for another book.

About Fast Arrow and the Forgotten Ones

This book represents the messages of my Home Circle during the Covid-19 pandemic in 2020.

A trance control medium has several guides or teachers who speak or heal through him. These spirit guides come in groups, but the medium normally does not recognize all of them, because that would hinder the work of the medium in a trance. There is usually one speaker in every group who gives the messages of the whole spirit group.

My spirit guide team supports me in my work as a healing medium, and as a trance speaker, but also with Earth healing. I assume they also inspire me when I write books.

I perceive these energies of my spirit helper team during a session as a group in the form of warmth, changes in my body, or through the messages I receive. My sitters can see the different guides during my trance.

In this time of the Covid-19 pandemic, there were especially Native Americans, philosophers, and/ or healers on my side to share their wisdom and healing power.

My Indian spirit guide team calls itself a clan. The members of this clan once lived on this Earth when everything was still in harmony and peace. They love Mother Earth and take notice of what people in our generation do to her.

The Forgotten Ones want to help us on our way through these rough times, but they also want to help Mother Earth to protect our nature and environment and to make this Earth a better place. To find a way back to more harmony, empathy and humanity.

In my Wednesday Home Circle two Indians introduced themselves by name. They were new guides for me, or I first noticed them for the first time consciously in a trance.

The first one was "Fast Arrow". He was an American Indian with a feather headdress. I guess I saw him before in my shamanic work, but not so clearly as in my first trance sitting. Fast Arrow painted an Indian arrow with my left hand during my trance speaking audibly to show clearly what he wanted to communicate. This was in body trance control with the hand I never write or paint.

The next spirit guide to show up was also a North American Indian. He called himself "White Feather". This was very touching for me, as I had some special experiences with white feathers in my life, and for me these were always messages of my deficiency in protection. But maybe it was already a sign and greeting from my guide White Feather.

I had a special feather experience about 15 years ago during a hike in the Taunus mountains in Germany. I was walking in a valley at the edge of the forest when suddenly and quickly a heavy storm came up. I knew that the way along the forest to the car was too far, and that I couldn't get there in time.

I continued my way in the direction of the parking lot, which led to fenced allotments, which were as deserted as the hiking trail. Suddenly a little white feather was floating in front of me. It did not float to the ground, but flew on and on in front of me, the way I went. Then suddenly this feather landed very gently on the trail. This made me look around, because to me it was a sign from my angels. And so I found that the feather had landed right in front of a garden gate with a sign attached. This sign said that this was a private path into the village that you could walk at your own risk. So I was able to walk straight through these allotments and get to the car without any detours. The moment I got into the car, the storm started with lightning and thunder, and heavy rain poured onto the valley and the car.

I got goose pimples and was immensely grateful to my spiritual support team for showing me this shortcut.

Further experiences followed with white feathers.

There were also touching feather experiences during the first time of the Wednesday Home Circle. In the early days of the Home Circle feathers showed up or sometimes even materialized in different places. The first quill was suddenly in my waiting room under a participant's chair. A short time later she informed me that she could not attend the meeting that evening. At that time she was very grieved personally and only a few days later wrote to me that a feather had appeared in her house as if out of nowhere. She found this feather in a room that was locked all week.

In the afternoon, a patient also found a white feather on the floor in the living room, just as I was on a shamanic healing journey for a relative of hers that she was worried about. She reported that all the windows were closed, and that she had never had a feather in the room.

Our guides do not always show us so clearly that they are around, supporting and inspiring us. I am all the more grateful to my spiritual team that they have made themselves visible so often in my life, even in human form, so that I could not ignore them. They opened my eyes so often to other realities.

I understood that it is now up to me to do something for these guides and carry their messages out into the world on this path. May these words, received in trance control, touch many human hearts and open them to our Mother Earth.

I wish that one day humanity will once again live in harmony and peace with the Earth and with one another, as it was everyday life for the Fast Arrow Clan. Let us be inspired by their words and let us thus be carried through the storms of our time.

How it Began

We began our Home Circle on September 16th 2020 in Bad Homburg, Germany during the Covid-19 Pandemic.

I met some friends at these Wednesday evening meetings to connect with my spirit teams for trance control, to go further from mind control into body control like Steven Upton told me to do.

The number of participants in the circle changed in the following weeks due to the changing distance rules, especially during the contact restrictions on the occasion of the second wave of the Covid-19 pandemic. Sometimes only five or three people or only people from two households were allowed to meet. But the energy remained high, and the messages and trance sittings became deeper and deeper. Or rather, the connection with my guides became closer and more intensive. I needed to go inside myself to evolve my trance mediumship during this time, just as the virus asked us to go inside at the time when it was forbidden to go out. The messages of my spiritual team often had to do with this special time, but they also answered the questions of participants or provided them with healing energies to go through these times.

Soon I recognized that this Home Circle was not only there to develop my trance abilities. It was a sacred time to get to know ourselves and learn from the spirits, not only trance.

They never gave healing recipes. Perhaps this was so because they know that as a non-medical practitioner in Germany I am not allowed to treat Covid-19 patients. But this is not what this book is about.

As soon as I was in trance control, the first North American Indian spoke to us, Fast Arrow. The Indian arrow was a symbol for bringing the messages to a point, to be specific. It was also a symbol for its Indian ancestry. The attendees saw that my face was changing while I was speaking. It got wrinkled.

Unexpectedly I spoke English in trance even though it was a German group. And this continued in the following weeks. I passed on my trance messages in English, even if the participants did not understand it.

Maybe because the guides were American, and it was their language? Or because the energy of these words was different in English than in German? For me the energy of the name "The Forgotten Ones" has a different vibration than the German translation "Die Vergessenen". May be this was the reason for it? Or maybe they delivered their words in English because these messages wanted to be carried beyond the German borders?

In these trance sittings the participants saw not only this face of an Indian, with brown skin and long hair. They also saw the faces of scholars, philosophers. Men and women.

My aura changed. Often I was not visible to the participants, as if I were behind a veil. Or the aura turned bright white, especially my arms and hands. Many participants saw this, even those who had never seen anything like this before, and who were most amazed about it. The sitters saw this white energy especially when my guides let healing energy flow through my hands. I felt this energy, but did not see it. It got more from week to week. It was hot, tickled and vibrated. It was as if a ball of energy was forming in my hand. My guides confirmed this and called it a ball of energy through which I would heal.

One participant saw a spirit guide emerge from my throat when I spoke in a trance for the first time at this Wednesday circle on September 16, 2020.

At the first circles I feared I did not speak in trance, but I felt the presence of the spiritual teachers in my aura and I got their message like a download. And the sitters felt and saw these spirit guide teams, saw them even more clearly than I did.

I was sure that my guides were there, as I had felt it for months in my development circle, and they inspired me to trust in myself and our connection and encouraged me to speak. And so I did.

Before these first words I saw an Indian head with a large feather headdress.

Two of the three participants also saw this American Indian and knew he wasn't from our time.

This Indian said that they were a "spirit guide group" as I had learned. However, he called it clan. And he said he was the spokesman of that clan. He also felt like a chief to me.

He said they were like stars in the firmament. Each a single star with a task, but connected like a star sign. They all shine in their own way, with their individual qualities. They are individual personalities, yet connected for a higher purpose. They are connected to one another and together have a special power. This can be compared to the zodiac sign, Leo, Libra or Pisces. And that's exactly how we should live. He said we should work in this way also with our soul family. Support each other and not compare. Not be jealous.

Then the participants were told to feel the Earth beneath their feet to find the connection to Mother Earth again. He said they lived in harmony with the Earth. People have lost this harmony in our times.

He said several times that they were grateful that we were there in this circle. Especially in these turbulent, chaotic times. And he assured us that they would support us from „over there" - from „their side of life".

And then he sent light to the participants. My hands "glowed" and got very hot, and I felt a kind of ball of light in my left hand.
When I had finished the trance speaking the participants saw the Forgotten Ones go away and my aura changed again, it became normal, without rays, wrinkles or such things, it was and felt like before.

And here is a report from a participant of this first touching Home Circle meeting on September 16, 2020 in my practice:

„My first SITTING
I doubted that I could just sit quietly for so long and watch in silence ... But these thoughts were unnecessary because it was exciting from the start.
It wasn't easy to focus my gaze on Diana, but I managed to block out everything else and fix myself fully on her face, and when it started, the first OHHHHH came, because the moment she went into a trance, I saw faces on her face!
There were a few different faces, an old woman, an Indian, a man with a top hat, and another woman who at first scared me a bit, because she had red eyes with which she looked at me, and because these faces were so alive ... but then I calmed down a bit, because I recognized that the person who Diana was communicating with appeared on her face, and the red eyes were the friendly smiling eyes of the red Earth goddess herself ❤ the change.

It was fascinating and exciting to watch, it seemed as if everyone had something to say, and it was more than I thought, because at the beginning they changed quickly and during the trance they usually stayed a moment before the next "speaks". At some point Diana began to write, at least it looked like that, unfortunately I didn't notice what she looked like when she was writing, because I was blown away by the fact that she moved her hand and fingers as if she was writing and painting.

It went on like this for a long time and the faces kept changing, and the red eyes of the Earth goddess beamed lovingly at me. ❤ Towards the end it was like the beginning, the faces changed quickly as if everyone wanted to say goodbye and then Diana was fully with us again.

In the conversation afterwards I got the confirmation that I hadn't imagined that. ❤

I'm looking forward to the next time!"
G. N.

The Forgotten Ones Speak

I am reproducing the original messages from the Forgotten Ones that I recorded during the Home Circle. Already that evening I couldn't remember all that had been said.

Trance Speaking September 23, 2020

These times are special. Full of grace and blessings. And full of possibilities.

We are like your stars. Shining from the heavens. You can follow us like the Northern Star. You do not need to do it, but it can help. This can help through dark times and fears.

These are special times. Full of growing. Let it go. You can be like a star for others or can help them on their way. Take your soul star. Follow your way in these times. We are here with you. Helping you. Guiding you. You are not alone in this time. Follow your star.

We are here as healers, as guides. Inspirations. To help you to go forward. Don't stop in fear or hate. Do not let the fear of others enter your heart and your soul. Go your own way. Believe in yourself, in your soul, your star and your guides.

Everyone has a guide at his side. They shine your way.

Do not follow the path of others. Find yours. Your own path into your life. And shine to others.

We are here to support, bless, heal you. But you live your life. We can show you ways, possibilities, help, but you have to live your life.

Feel the pulse of the Earth under your feet. Connect with Mother Earth. With her energy. Trust Mother Earth. Your connection to Mother Earth.

We send you light for growth. Cover yourselves with it. Maybe you can feel the warmth. The light. You are not alone.

Do not compare yourself with others. No star compares with another star. Every star has a place in this universe. Full of light. Space. But humans do not understand this. They compare their life with other lives. Do not compare a rose and a daisy. Everyone has a place in this universe. A place with love. Do not compare.

Maybe you can reach a mountain. Maybe not. Everyone has his own vision. You do not know what another person's life plan is. Do not compare their lives with yours. Follow your way, your vision.

We send you healing now. Feel the healing energy in your heart. Now. We send healing.

You can go through stormy times like the buffalo. He will not be stuck in fears. He goes into the storm. He knows the storm will pass on.

The buffalo doesn't run away from the storm. He goes into the storm and through the storm. So you can go through this time. Don't run away and freeze in fear.

The buffalo faces the storm. And the storm passes faster than you think.

Do not dig too deep into your problems. Sometimes the solution is at the end of the roots, but not always. Sometimes you dig too deep in your life. Like a flower concentrate on the sun above you, not on the roots where you think your problems are. Sometimes you dig too deep. You see problems where there are none. You are looking for problems that never will turn up.

Be like a flower to the sun. To the healing lights. To your angels, guides, stars. And not to your problems.

You need strong roots in your family. When you do not have these roots, build your own roots. Your connection to Mother Earth. To your soul family and friends. To Nature. That helps.

But do not concentrate on this all the time.

Don't forget the sun, the stars, the life energy above you. The healing lights.

We help you to heal and to live.

Not only do you have to learn, we also have to learn to work with you. To find the voice inside of you. For our world.

We learn together. We heal together. But it needs time. To develop. To grow. To connect.

We have to learn it on both sides. Every human is different. Everyone learns differently. We have to learn together. And to connect. To go forward. Give us time. To grow and heal. To grow to the sun, to the light. Like a flower we will grow to the light inside you and above you.

Reports of the Participants of this Circle

„*I saw less than I felt. Diana's body was framed by a bright, glistening light (I found it pleasant), like the layer of an aura. On the right side (her actual right side) the layer was significantly thicker, especially from the shoulder to the crown chakra. A strong energy flowed which I felt in my body, so that my legs sometimes twitched without my being able to stop it. It was pleasantly warm, and I felt safe.*"
B. T.

„*I think the first time I suddenly panicked and had bad breath ... I started to fidget, got restless, my legs suddenly hurt ... I saw a bright light behind Diana and got goose bumps, because I felt that someone was walking past me from behind, but there was nobody there ... I went home, very exhausted, and the next day I felt really good ...*"
C. S.

„*Before the first session, I was a little nervous, because I didn't know what to expect. I didn't notice anything for the first few minutes, but I enjoyed the silence. Then when Diana started speaking, everything changed in my head.*

At first I thought I was concentrating too much on being quiet ... but it wasn't that. I saw a kind of fog in the room where Diana was sitting, I kept opening and closing my eyes to check whether the appearance was still there; it was real, the "two sitters" who were still sitting in the room were completely gone for me ... Instead of seeing them I perceived Diana's head as in a flip book, in a grid scheme. I saw different faces that kept appearing. There was a kind of Indian, without a headdress, but with face paint. A woman Diana's age but with three times the amount of hair. When that woman's face appeared, I felt as if someone behind Diana had switched the light on and off.

My body was magically drawn to ... something ... When Diana stopped talking, everyone was gone. My body felt light and somehow "new", but also like "discharged"?! I slept like a bear that night."

S. L.

Find Your Truth

Trance Speaking September 30, 2020

Your time is like a flower in the spring who wants to grow, but people do not let it grow.

Like a little flower full of energy, power, life force, coming through the Earth to new life, but people do not let it grow.

Your life is like a little flower in the spring. New potential. New life. But people do not see it. They want to be stuck in the old energies, the things they know. But they have to go forward to a new life. Full of peace, love, gratitude, friendship, brotherhood. A new life in peace. This flower is on the way. But many people do not think that it grows. Do not let it grow. They are full of hate and fears.

What is growing in your life? What is new? Let this grow now. To a new life. Something in your life that you always wanted to do. To learn. To write. To paint.

Like the crop. The seeds are put in the Earth in the winter time. They are lying in the ground, and there is still nothing to be seen. It is waiting for you let it grow. Grow.

We send you healing light and peace. Feel it in your heart, body and your mind. Let it grow like a flower that comes out of the snow. It brings hope, peace and life.

You are like this flower and should not give up. In dark and cold times do not give up and grow towards the sun and the stars.

We are here from the old times. The Forgotten Ones. We are the Indians, from the Earth, nature, sun and stars. We are the Forgotten Ones, but we are still here. We love the land. The flower. The trees. The stars.
Not only we are forgotten. Nature is forgotten. We are the forgotten.
We want to help in peace. To live in peace.
All is living. The Earth, the stars, the seas, the animals and the flowers.
We are here to help you to go through these times towards a new Earth in peace.
The buffalo goes to the storm. We will help you through this storm this time.
It will be a storm. More than you believe. But we will help you through this time.
We are the Forgotten Ones, but we are still here.

We are the healers of this Earth and your soul. Feel the energy in your soul and your heart. We are here to heal you and your soul. Feel it.

Like the snail and the soul. Find the patience and the soul inside yourself. Find the answers in yourself.
Go into your heart and your soul. Do not believe in others.

Find it in your own soul. We help you with this. Like the snail which goes into its house. Learn to go into yourself. Every day. Every week. As it is possible for you.

Do not look for the truth outside yourself. Go inside and find it in your heart. We help you to find it.

Go into your heart and feel the truth. Not into your mind. People want to control your mind. Your brain. But come into your heart and feel the truth in this world of life. We can help you to find the truth.

The truth does not belong to the loudest man. You can find it in nature. In the trees. The animals. The spirits. They are not loud. You have to find them. They are waiting for you. Go to nature and find the truth.

We send you healing energy now. Feel the energy from our world. From us, the forgotten. We are still here and you can feel us through this energy. We are still here.

We send the healing energy through the times of your life. Like layers inside of you. Layers that need help and healing and trust and hope. What is not in balance? What is crying for help? Unseen? Bring it in harmony.

Everything has its place. Like the stars in heaven. Everything has a place in your life. Listen and trust.

It is time to go, but we will be here soon again. We believe in you. We protect you. We heal you and help you through these times.

Observations of the Participants

„This time I had great difficulty in concentrating/ focusing. I felt the energy even more than the first time. As a result, my legs twitched permanently and I felt a strong inner restlessness. But I didn't find it uncomfortable, more like too much energy, and as if I had to "let off steam". As last time, Diana was surrounded by the light already described on this evening. At the end of the session, an Indian (on her right) was standing behind her. That was the first time that I saw a "figure"."
B. T.

„The second time I was downright shocked and the other participants confirmed to me that I also said "wow" or something like that, because from Diana came an Indian face that came into the room ... and I unfortunately no longer know whether it was the first time or the second time that I just had to cry and didn't know why. For me it was a great experience when she talked about Mother Earth and the stars in English and once in German and scribbled on the pad."
C. S.

„The next Wednesday circle was different. I was calm from the start, completely relaxed. Nothing happened in the beginning. And again when Diana began to speak, an older man and an older woman appeared on her face. Both of them without hair or strictly set back. Type similar, Asian, Japanese something like that. Both very friendly. Always appearing alternately, always behind a bright light in purple - pink going around Diana's upper body. At the end there was a creature similar to a turtle head, very sensual and nice. Again I went home relaxed."

S. L.

„At the first meeting in which I participated, after about 15 minutes I had the impression of a strong burst of energy, it made me cry, it felt so moving. The words Diana spoke also touched me very much. During the session, I saw an Indian and a Mongol alternating on her face."

C. H.

The Space Between

Trance Speaking October 7, 2020

We are here to lead you through the storms and through the hard times. Difficult times. Sad times.

You think we are only here when you feel alone, full of fear. We are always here, but you are blind for our world when you are not in fear.

We meet in hard times, dark times, like those you are going through. The world is changing. People are changing. It's on you to change: you, the world inside you.

Look through the stars. But not at the stars: at the space between the stars. The energy. The energy between people, between things, between you and your neighbour.

It is the energy which changes things, not the person. It is like the atoms. You have forgotten that the energy is in the emptiness, not in what you see. But people do not understand it until now. It is far away from your mind to understand it. You have to feel it, not to understand it with your mind or brain. Feel the energy in the atoms, between the atoms. You and your friend, the family.

What can you feel between each other? Have you felt it, recognized it? It is about the energy.

There is more like this. It is energy. It is not easy to describe it to you.

We are working with the energy around you. Not in you. It is the magnetic field, energy. You can change it with your thoughts. With your heart. With your love.

It is the higher vibration you need, that we can work with you. Go from your mind into your heart.

See the ocean and the moon. How they react. People do not know the secrets behind. Feel the secrets with your heart. Go out of your brain into your heart. You can feel the truth in your heart. Feel the energy in your heart.

Like your organs. Do not always look at your kidneys, liver. Look at the space between. The body works, if all works together. When something is missing like with the stars in the sky: When a star is missing the energy is different. The stars, the signs. And so it is in your body. When something is missing the energy is different. You are different. You have to find something instead of what is missing. You will learn it, but not today. We will describe it, but not today. But understand your feelings, your heart. All is connected. And when something is missing, there is no harmony in your world and in your skies. When animals are missing there is no harmony like before. In your dimension they do not know what they are doing. In this world and nature, and with their bodies and all.

The harmony is gone. You have to look for it and bring it back to this world to have peace.

Colors and Vibrations

Trance Speaking October 14, 2020

We will move your hands for healing. We work through the aura field, the energy around the body. We work through your hands. The energy. All are here with the wisdom what is behind it, the things you see. Maybe you can feel it, when you are blind for the things. You have to feel it in your heart, with your soul. You can feel the energy around you, the energy of the body, of people. The energy is not constant. It is changing. Flowing. Everyday is unique. It's on you to find what is behind.

What is equal? What is not changing in the energies?

We see the colors of the soul. You too can see and feel them.

I send you now the light blue from the oceans. Feel it in your heart. It is cold. Wide. It is green.

We heal with light and colors and vibrations. Beyond all you can imagine. We heal behind time and space. You will learn it. But not today. It is all about learning with patience and trust.

We thank you for being here. To help to come back to each other. To find peace and healing in your soul.

Feel the energy we send to you. We send you healing now. Healing from far beyond your imagination. From our side of life. We send you light. From our side of life. Feel the energy around you.

Why are you here? What are you searching for? Peace? I am here at your side and asking why are you here? What do you need in your life? What are you looking for? How can we help, so that you are live in peace, freedom and joy?

People need to go inside to find the purpose of life. We are here to help and to open your heart. We send you energy to open your heart.

Our ancestors lived their lives in two worlds. Your culture has forgotten it. It is time to go inside, to find your roots and belief.

Trance Speaking October 21, 2020

We light your way through the darkness. We are here to give you peace, trust, patience. We give you light for the dark times. Full of fear, hate, jealousy. People don't look at their own way. They look at each other. Jealous of their way. Of all they have. Not trusting in themselves and their way. They should go their own way, without fear and with trust. We are here to help you through these dark times.

We know each other from long ago. We had this appointment to meet here. To bring peace and light and love. Into your own heart and into your way. For your own way. Don't look at the others. Don't let them change your way. Don't let them steal your faith and trust in yourself. Go your own way. Like the buffalo.

You have organs in your body that have higher frequency than others. You call them the important ones, but there is more than this. They have a higher frequency. And if they are missing the frequency of your body is not so high as it should be.
And what are you doing? You do not put it higher. You put it lower. You have to help in the frequency of this part of the body. With trust, love and patience.
We send high frequency, colors, healing. Higher than you think. We are here to help you through this. To heel and understand. This space between all, it is magnetic and high vibration. You have to learn what is behind. This takes time.

The lowest frequency is at your feet, on the ground, and it goes higher in the whole body to your head, like the chakra goes to a higher vibration, but you do not understand it. They take us to an upper and lower vibration than your heart and your lungs. Think about this. You can't heal them with the same vibration. It goes higher than the ears.
The brain is the highest. You have to think about it. Think about what is behind.

The Corona virus has some higher vibration. So it goes to the lungs. Not deeper. The lung has to be cured with higher vibrations like the brain. You have to think about it. It is different.

We send you healing now. We send you high vibrations of healing to your heart, to your lungs and brain. Feel this now. High vibrations of healing for the upper body. Can you feel it? And the colors blue, violet and white. Feel the high vibrations of healing in your heart, lungs, head. And green. And then lower vibrations for the lower body. Legs. Digestive system. Organs. Yellow. Red. Orange. Feel the difference between the vibrations now. It is not so high and fast. It is low. It has the connection to Mother Earth. Red.

Like the sun and the moon - they have different vibrations. Think about this.

A virus has a higher vibration than a bacterium. Think about it. It can change your life. Turn the vibration. But you have to learn from it.

We send you healing. We send you higher vibration of healing. For this times. But you have to uplift yourself to these vibrations to go through these times. Through meditation. Compassion and understanding. Empathy. Not hate and fear. People who are full of fear do not get through these times well. People who are full of hate. But they do not understand. They should go through these times with higher vibration.

We are the Forgotten Ones. Forgotten wisdom. People think they know it better now. They have forgotten the old wisdom and us.

They are looking for high vibrations and things. But are stuck in lower vibrations, full of jealousy, hate and all this.

We are the Forgotten Ones. And we are here to help you through these times with our light and wisdom. But trust in yourself and your heart. And go your way in these times, which are full of growing and change.

Like the Northern Star which stays at its place, trust in yourself in these times. When all is changing around you stay in your peace and trust.

Reports of the Participants

„The room was again filled with this pleasant, very strong energy that flowed through my body. This time I was able to concentrate well. The light surrounded Diana again, as in all sessions, always on her right side and in the same place more expanded / thicker. I could see several of her helpers, such as for example an angel, Mother Mary, a Chinese and again the Indian."
B. S.

„At the third Wednesday Circle I arrived at the practice with massive pain in the back and a tense body. At the beginning, as always, nothing happened, I was just concerned about whether I could sit quietly with this pain.
Diana started to talk, I suddenly had the feeling as if someone was touching me and kept stroking this place, on the neck, on the back of my neck and on the right side of my body.
I didn't see any faces this time. I just felt a strange feeling in my body. It was as if someone was "working" on or in me. But actually I somehow didn't feel my body.

A "glow" kept coming up on Diana's larynx, but only when she wasn't speaking.
In the end I was completely free of pain all over my body, I felt good, but I was completely exhausted, like after a day's hike."
S. L.

Balloon of Wishes

Trance Speaking October 28, 2020

We are here from the Other Side of life, the Forgotten Ones. We know ourselves. We thank you for being here and talking to us.

We are the Forgotten Ones. In these dark times people have to trust themselves. In the light inside themselves. Not in the light of others. They should not follow others like the Northern Star. Like a ship. You should not follow the other people. You don't know, if you can trust them like the Northern Star. This star will never change, but people change, especially in these times. They are not like the Northern Star.

They change their opinion. They change their believes. They change their life styles, to be something special. Trust in yourself and in your heart. And you can trust in the Northern Star. These are the Forgotten Ones. Your guides. But people do not trust us anymore. They have forgotten us. They think they have new lives, and they fail. Believe in yourself. Trust yourself and go your way. Go inside yourself. You will find inner worlds that can show you your way. Inspiration. Your life purpose. Your inner star.

Do not trust and believe in the loudest people. Believe in yourself.

We send you peace and healing. Green light of healing for your heart. To find this trust and believe yourself. Feel the light of healing for your heart. We send it now.

Green light for your heart. Fill your heart with this.

Don't be afraid of these dark and hard times. Trust in yourself and your spirit guides. They show you a way through these dark times. With their inner light and healing power.

Go away from people you cannot trust. Go into your own power inside yourself. We are waiting there for you. With our love and light and inspiration on our side.

We send you white light from the heavens. To heal the soul. We surround you with this.

And the golden light from the heavens. Like a golden star. Shimmering. Wrap yourself inside this light, to go through these times.

Take care of yourself.

Dreams are endless if you want. You can dream them to an end – to a happy end, if you want.

You can lose yourself in your dreams or you can make them real. What do you choose?

Do you want to stay a dreamer? Or do you want to create your dreams? A happy ending.

We help you with this.

Go inside your dreams. See the purpose, your wishes, and dream them to reality.

Dream your life happy, your health will be good. Your partnership lovely. Family is lucky. All that you want.

But people dream their lives in a bad way. The circumstances are bad.

Allow your dreams to turn into reality. We help you with this. Like a balloon you can put them inside. You can put them in the air. You can let them fly. You have to let them become true.

Put your wishes in this balloon. Like the times in your childhood - let them flow. Full of hope and happiness and joy. With excitement that comes. Where will they land? They will find their way and land. Let it be and let it become true.

We are the Forgotten Ones. We are here to teach you the old wisdom. The old ways of living. In peace with nature and each other. Peace between people.

You should live like the trees. Together, but on your own.

Trees do not compare with each other. They let the other trees grow their way.

They communicate with others. But they do not behave like humans, full of jealousy and hate.

We are the Forgotten Ones. We are here. We met before. We wanted to meet in these times. To learn from each other. To help each other through these storms. We tried it before. But it failed. Every time it failed. People failed.

Through this time and nature. This planet. And then to the stars.

And then no one can understand what they are doing. They think they do not need each other. But in this world everything has its place. It only works together. You cannot have a forest with two or three trees. There is a connection. Like a family, like a nation, like a world. They do not understand.

Look inside your body. Everything works together like a nation. Everyone, everything has its place. Nothing is better than the other. The heart, the kidney, the lungs. Everything should work in harmony. Also in your world. People do not live in this harmony.

We send you peace and harmony and healing light. Green. Turquoise. Let it into your heart and into your soul. We send you healing now. Believe in yourself and in your community. Build your own community. Begin with a little one and let it grow. A place of light in these dark times. People who help each other. Without jealousy and hate. May your dreams become reality.

The virus is here to help, to bring people together, not apart. People are going apart in this time. That is not the way it should be. The virus will not go away before people learn this. They have to take care of each other, not to fight. The virus is here to bring peace, not hate.

We are the Forgotten Ones.

Take care of yourself and the world around you. Find a time for yourself and meditate and find the peace in yourself and bring it to other people.

You think you are not able to do that, that you are too small. But you are able to do this. Begin with small things and let it grow higher. Bigger.
You do not know what you can do and what would be missing if you were not here. Believe in yourself and your wishes.
We met before, and we had an appointment to meet here in these times. You will soon understand it.
It is a time to go inside, and you will find us. We will meet here. Believe it and do not fear.

We send you healing and light. We wish you a good time, and we will see each other again.
Take care of this world and each other and your dreams.
Soon you can ask questions. We can talk to each other about these times.
Now it is time to go. We thank you from our heart and we will meet again. Take care of yourself and this world.

Find Your Roots

Trance Speaking November 4, 2020

We are here, the Forgotten Ones. We are here from the light within you and outside of you. We are here in these dark times to bring you this light to your consciousness far beyond your imagination. This light is deep within you. It has a high vibration of love, trust, belief. Believe in the good things. Believe in humanity. Believe in your own soul star. We are here to guide you through this storm, with this light within you. We will touch you deep in your heart with this light. Now we send you this light deep into your heart. Green light from our world. From our side of life. Feel it in your heart. It will guide you through these storms. We give you peace, healing and trust in yourself and in our world and in your heart. Feel the green light we send you now.
It is the green of the oceans and the forests. Nature in harmony, full of life, peace and love and energy.

Believe in yourself and your way. Do not trust other people, their opinion too much. Find the truth in your heart to go through these storms and dark times.

We are the Forgotten Ones. People could take our wisdom through these times. Like the soul star, the Northern Star, as we told you before. People do not trust us anymore. People think they have the wisdom in themselves. But they do not look into their heart, into their soul. They think they find it in their brain. But there is not the inspiration, it is their ego and this can't help through these storms.

Go inside yourself. Meditate and find the wisdom in your heart, in your soul and not in your brain.

Your soul will live forward, it does not die. It knows the old wisdom.

Take the wounds of your heart. Heal them with our light. So that you find the wisdom behind it. The forgotten wisdom.

We send you healing light now. The yellow light of joy in your solar plexus. Joyful times, like the sun. Life force. We send you this. The warm energy of the sun. People have forgotten to live in joy and peace. Everyone wants to be better than the other one. Everyone wants to be the best. Everyone wants to have the higher wisdom. Everyone wants to be the best. They are self-confident, but fail in what they think and do. They fail and bring no freedom to people. They bring hate, no empathy. The world shows what people behave like. There is no harmony in the weather, in nature, among the animals. Parts of nature disappear. There is an extinction in nature and emotions.

Be like the whale in the ocean, full of trust, old wisdom and patience. Not like the fox in the forest, full of jealousy.

We send you healing light and trust.

People have forgotten where they come from. They have forgotten their roots. They do not look for their roots. They look at the stars, but they don't understand the stars. They think they find their star family outside of their world, outside of them. But that's not true. You can find us in yourself. In your roots, in this Earth. They think they have a high vibration, but this is a deep vibration of hate and jealousy. You cannot find the freedom outside of yourself and the stars. The stars can help you to find your way inside of yourself which you have forgotten.

Our ancestors are here to help you through these times. You can find them in Mother Earth, in nature and inside yourself. Not in the stars.

You have guides in the stars, from the star family, from the heavens, but this is not the same. They can help you, but you need your roots, your connection with Mother Earth. We are not sitting on Venus or on Mars. There are energies, not your guides. They are inside your heart, waiting for you. People have forgotten the old ways of living in peace and harmony with this Earth. They come to find it in the stars. We will help you and we begin now.

You have energy in your body, which circulates through your body from your feet to the head and above. This energy can be clear, dark, full of anger, or fear. You have to clear this energy in yourself and around you. We can help you with this.

We can send you energy and power to clean your own power. Begin in your heart. Fill your heart with this energy. Light, peace and love. We send you green energy of life from nature. Fill your heart with this energy and heal it with this. And from there, from this place in your heart you can let it circulate through your body. We send you green light now. It is full of trust and faith in your roots and life. People have forgotten this.

Fill your heart with this light and let it heal. Bring faith into this light with the green light.

I am Fast Arrow and I come from a time far away from this.

This virus brings you a new understanding of life. How things work together. All is connected. You cannot live your life at your own. People think they can. They are egoistic. They look for their way, for their best.

But the virus shows you, you cannot live on your own. All is connected. You can heal it, not on your own. But people do not understand. They do not want to change. They do not want to grow in the right direction.

They do not want to change anything they do not want. But the virus will change like the people. It will not go away by ignorance.

We are here to help you through these times. To turn in the right direction, for a better world. You need to have trust, patience and belief.

We send you healing light to grow and to fulfill your soul plan and your vision. We wish you high visions like the stars. Fulfill them with your connection to Mother Earth and us.

You are like a bird who wants to fly. You have to move out of your fears, spread your wings and fly. Trust yourself. We can help you with this. You can fly. Don't get stuck. Fly with the winds of empathy and love and the wisdom inside of you. Fly.
Everything begins with a first step, you know. Look at this little bird, at its first flight. It need not be perfect. But you have to start your vision to come true. Believe in your vision and fly.
You will be stronger, you will have more faith and success, but you have to do the first flight from this tree in the world. Trust yourself and fly. The shyest ones sit in their trees and do not fly.
It is time to go into this world to share your wisdom. Your love. There is a vision to share. Believe in yourself. Start to fly. Spread your wings.

In these days and these times you are not alone. Ask for our help when you are in fear or feeling alone.
You are never alone, we are all with you. We guide you through these times with our light. Ask for it, and we will be here.

Thank you for being here with your light. We met before. We wanted to meet now. Believe in our connection, in our vision together. To create peace on Earth and healing. With forces of light, we are here together. Never forget this in these times. We are here. We go with you to show you the way in these times.
Thank you.

Spread Your Wings

Trance Speaking November 11, 2020

We are here from the Other Side of life. We are here to lead you through the storms. We help you in this time to trust, to keep your faith and your love.

We are the Forgotten Ones. And we want to help you through this time, full of storms. It is a time full of jealousy and hate. People are full of anger. We help you through this.

Do not take this time for granted. Take nothing for granted in this world. Everything was too granted. Freedom. Life. Nothing is like before. People miss their freedom, their old life. But it's gone. It is not possible to step back. We have to go forward into a better world. But people look back. They want to have their old lives back. But they have to change like the Earth. With trust and empathy. We are here to help you, but people are deaf for us. They do not hear us anymore. They think they know it better than us, the Indians.

We send you healing into your heart. Energy of trust, hope and light. Feel it in your heart and take it in this time.

We make an energy ball full of light and healing energy for you. With the feeling of freedom for the soul.

You are still sitting in your tree like a bird unable to fly. You think you are not able to fly. But you can fly. You have to go forward, a step into an uncertain future. There is no ground beneath you. You have to fly. Don't look back. Fly!

Make the best of this time and the best of yourself. Be the bird that trusts and flies. We help you with this. We are your winds, that help you to fly. We send you blue light of trust, calmness, courage. Fly with these winds of change. Don't look back and do not look down. Only look forward to a better world that will come. Don't look back!

We send you this blue light now. Energy and trust. We send it into your heart and your soul.

You can ask something. Do you want to ask something?

Question: Can you tell us your name?
Answer: Fast Arrow.

Question: Where do you come from?
Answer: From far behind this time. Far from this world, from another world. When all was in peace. People lived in peace with nature in the old times in America. We are Indians. And we love Mother Earth like you do.

Question: Are you alone? Or a lot?
Answer: We are a clan. We are more than you think. Ten of us are here.

Question: What can we do to heal Mother Earth?
Answer: Go into your heart. Live in your heart. Don't compare yourself with others. Fill Mother Earth with your love and light and passion. We are like a sunbeam that shines into the darkest places of this Earth. Send your light in the darkest places like the sun.

Question: What can we do to heal our family?
Answer: Be the sunbeam. Shine. Give them trust, happiness, do not think too much. Do not take everything for granted and do not compare. And do not take things too personally. It is not always about you. You think it is about you, but it is not all about you. Do not take it too your heart too personally. Go a step back to see the bigger picture of the family and life. It is not about you. It's about the whole.

Question: Can you tell me something about the way of my life? What can I do to go my way?
Answer: Trust in yourself and be the bird that flies. Don't stuck in. Don't think too much. You think too much. You have to trust in yourself and your way. You can give people much, your wisdom, your love. But you have to do it. And do not think too much. Do it!

Question: What can I do to heal my legs?
Answer: Don't think so much. Go your way. Your legs want to go in another direction. You have to let them go.

You stop yourself. Ask your legs where they want to go. Did you do this? You have to speak to your legs. Ask them where they want to go and when they want to rest.

Questioner: Thank you that you come to us and help us.
Answer: Thank you for being here. Be the bird which flies, and you do not need your legs. You can fly. Follow your visions and fly. You stop yourself. You all could fly. We send you the healing light to fly, to trust yourself. Be this light.
See the fish in the sea. They don't see the whole. They do not see what is above them. They think that the water and their environment is all that exists. Don't be like these fish. See the world above and more that exists. You are on your way. You are looking for other universes, wisdom. Go forward and learn what's behind. Trust yourself.
You are living like a fish that is swimming and does not need legs. But it is time to use your legs to go in the right direction. And then they will heal.
Ask your legs and your soul where they want you to go. What do you want to do? And this will heal.
What do you want to do? Meditate about this. Ask where you want to go on your feet in this world. And go there. And find the peace and the wisdom. Not in the forests and not in the sea. Look where it is, this wisdom.
And do not hide yourself in the stars. There you do not need your legs either. You have to walk on this Earth. Do not dream yourself away from this Earth.

Question: Can I hope that my legs are so good that I can go to the woods and walk and walk and walk? For an hour or two?

Answer: You can go to the woods. But why to the woods? Ask your legs where they want to go.

Question: I like the trees. What can we do for the trees? They are ill.

Answer: Dream it in a better world. They have to go. You are not responsible for this. You have to let things go. You have to let things happen. It is not on to you. You did all you can, but some things happen.

So why do you go to the woods? Ask yourself where you have to go.

Don't hide yourself in the woods. Go into the world to share your wisdom, and not into the woods. Think about this. We are here to help you through this, but it is not all on us to change. You can't change everything, even if it hurts.

We love Mother Earth and the woods, but people do not have respect for nature. They have to respect our Mother Earth, then she will change and heal. But people do not see it. They only look at their own lives. What they lose in their lives. Not what Mother Earth is losing. They are blind for this.

We are the Forgotten Ones, and they have forgotten us like Mother Earth.

Do not be like a bird which sits in the tree, in the woods and which thinks it is secure. Nothing is secure. What will you do when the woods are gone? When the tree is gone? Where will you sit?

You have to find new visions. You have to fly. Fly where your legs want to be, and then you can land there.

Stand there. You can make a shamanic journey to this. You can see yourself in these woods. Fly like a bird and then look were you are landing. You have to find this place for yourself. And you will wonder where this will be, where this place is. And all can heal. But do not stay on this tree. The tree will be gone. And then? You better fly. Even if you do not want to hear this. This is true, the truth. Fly. Find a place for your legs and your feet and send your roots to Mother Earth and help this world to heal.

You cannot do nothing in this world. Everything is in needs in this world. If you are stuck and fear, it will not help anyone anything in this world. It is on you to go forward. Not to stuck.

Feel the wind of change. Spread your wings and fly. Do not stuck. Go forward. Fly.

Now we are sending you healing to fly. Inspiration, courage, trust. Feel it in your arms and your legs. We are sending you healing into your legs. Into your arms and into your heart. Feel this power for change. We will help you with this, but you have to fly.

Where do you want to go in this time?

Feel the power and energy and light, white light. Feel it.

Strong light to help, to heal you all. Trust in this light and feel this light.

Sometimes there is nothing more to do than this, to stand in the light and to shine your light.

You always want to do something. Sometimes you only have to stand there and send your light.

You do not need to go into the forest for this. Send it and stand for the light.

Sometimes it is enough. And you need this light in these times, that people stand for it.

Do not fall apart in the darkness and the hate. So many people fall apart. They are full of hate and darkness. They think they fight for the light. But this is not true. There is no light. They spread darkness and hate, no light!

Stand for this light. We need you for this. Send this light to the oceans and into nature. Around this Earth, and believe in it. Let it grow, and clear and transform. Look at the new life.

Questioner: We thank you for your healing and for your light.

Answer: We thank you for your light. You all. Thank for being here, for talking to us.

Make your heart light, like a feather. Let it fly. Where should it go?

Sometimes there is nothing to do. Only trust and fly with your vision.

Give up all your fears, darkness, pain and grief. Make your heart free and light. And you can fly like this feather in the wind. Like a message of God. From the angels.

It is time to heal. Your vision can help.
Do not forget the bird in the tree. Do not forget to fly. Do not forget your vision and your potential.
Do not think yourself small and weak. Think yourself strong and full of power. Self-confident. And then go and fly. And be the best vision of yourself, the best version of yourself. You can do this. But you have to start and fly.

Do not look at that dark clouds above you, underneath you. Look at the future, at the light. Fly. And change this world into a better place. Believe in this. You can help us with this and we thank you for this.
We are the Forgotten Ones, and we hope that this place, this Earth will be sacred again. But people have to change.

The Message of the Virus

Trance Speaking November 18, 2020

We are the Forgotten Ones. We are here with the energy of love, freedom, empathy. We are here to guide you through the storms without hate, only love. We hope you will try to fly, spread your wings and go with the wind of changes. But without war and hate.

We are here from the Other Side of life, from the ancient times. Masters of peace. We are here to help you to find this peace and wisdom and love.

Send your dreams to the highest places you can't imagine to reach. To the highest wisdom, the highest energies. This time will change people, not all for the better, also if they believe so. They want to change this Earth and society. Like they think it should be. It's in their mind, not in their heart. They criticize everything that is old. They want to create a new Earth energy but they fail. They have forgotten the old good energies. They ignore Mother Earth. They only look for their best, what kind of society they want to have. Not what's best for this Earth and all beings. Not only humans. They think they are so enlightened. But they walk in dark clouds and dark thoughts and dark behavior.

They think this is light, but it isn't. They think they are the "Chosen Ones", they think they are better than others, but that's not right. They do not have respect for the Earth, for all beings, for Brotherhood of Man. They think they can play God, but this will fail. They miss the tipping point.

We are here to help you through the times that will come. Hard times. But you can stand it, make it. Believe in yourself and your power and your love.

Be the peace in this world.

Life is like a forest. People think the strongest ones will survive. But that's not true. The forest survives together. All is connected. The trees, the animals.

Nothing is better than the other. Everything is needed. Give yourself this peace and trust and think of yourself as part of the wholeness of life. Nothing is better than the other.

We send you healing light to trust in yourself and the whole. People do not trust one another. They are looking for the worst things.

Feel the light of love and healing we send you now.

People do not have respect. They think they are better and the "Chosen Ones", and we are the Forgotten Ones. In our land people lived together in peace. Everyone was thankful for the other. A clan to be as one.

Everyone lived their visions for higher things. We are here to help you through this.

We were thankful for all that Mother Earth gave to us. We were thankful for nature, for the food, for the elements, the air that we breathed. The water we drank. The Earth. The wind. All was in harmony, and we lived with this harmony, with these elements, and in peace with nature, with the animals, with this Earth. These times are gone. People look for themselves. They live for their will. They have forgotten to be thankful. They don't give the Earth anything back. They only want to have more and more. But there is not enough there for their wishes.

The Earth needs healing.

People have to stop their old lives, their old way of life. But they are angry that the virus has stopped their way of life. They want to have their old lives back. But this will not happen. They are angry and full of hate. But anger prevents them from understanding what the Covid-19 virus tells the world, and what Mother Earth is telling them. They have to learn and they will learn, but this will take time.

We are here to teach you, to help you through this.

Feel the peace in your heart when you are in nature, at the ocean and in the forest.

Think about it, what gives you peace? What's there? Think about it.

It's not the material world you are longing for. It is dead. Nature is alive with energy and power. This empowers you, this lifts you up. This energy and life.

But you kill this energy and life and the whole world. So you will not find peace and rest. But people do not understand.

We send you green power of nature and energy, feel it in your heart. We heal you now with this power.

Feel it now. We fill your whole body with this energy of life and power of Mother Earth. To thank you for being here, for your heart. Feel this healing power of Mother Earth.

The virus will be there to teach people, but they are blind. It's about staying together, standing up for each other. Make a break for Mother Earth.

There will be a time better than this after this darkness. There will come light and joy. But this takes time. People need to remember their purpose of life. Why are you here? To have fun? Money? Or to find the love in everything that lives. Your passion. Empathy for all. To find your peace in this world. What's your passion? Your vision? Your dream? Meditate about this.

What can you give this world that nobody else can do? What is your place in this world? You will find it. Fly to this place.

You can ask me something. Do you have questions? You can ask in German.

Question: Where does the storm come from that opposes us?
Answer: These are the emotions of all people. They are the storm. They are attacking themselves.

They do not see what they are doing, what they are creating. Like a demon which does not exit.

They change everything. They change the climate.

They change the energy of the Earth and between people.

They have destroyed the peace in themselves and in this world. Nature, the storms, they reflect themselves.

They have to heal themselves. Their wounds, their emotions. But they act like hurricanes which destroy everything that gets in their way. There is no empathy. None!

Question: Where does the corona virus come from?

Answer: Do you really want to know it? Better not!

It's not relevant where it comes from. It is relevant why it comes! It's better to think about this. It's like the daemons mankind create. They created their virus. It's life that's out of control. It plays with mankind, with people. The playing game.

Whether it comes from a laboratory or nature is not important to know. Better not to know that. Don't fix on this. The virus is here, what does it wants to teach you? Why is it here?

People think they develop. They think they get better and better. Their technology gets better just like the virus. It develops like the people do. Everything is in a state of development. But not everything for its best.

The whole evolution is developing. It's like a mirror - the virus. And now it is out of control. The development of the virus and mankind. It's hard to stop. Everything will be better.

People are playing God. Sometimes there is a point of no return. You have to change this. Your behavior. This Earth, nature, the planet. The virus is a mirror of your society. The development of mankind. That's all.

May be it comes from a laboratory or from nature. It is not important where this development starts, but it's nearly out of control.

We are the Forgotten Ones. People say we are primitive, because we do not develop like you. But what's the right way? What's healthy? And what's heaven made? And what's man made? Think about this! You have to think a long time about this. And then you will understand the virus. Think about this. This is all I can say. And all I want to say.

We send you blue light of calmness to your soul. To find freedom, to take a break and heal inside of you.
Feel this blue light in your body and your soul.
Feel the blue light. Feel it in your stomach. Solar plexus. Your heart. Feel the calmness and the peace. It's needed here in this world. All this is missing in this pandemic. It is all about this.

Question: Should people get vaccinated against this virus, against Covid-19? Is it good for people?
Answer: This not the way to treat this virus. But it is not on us to answer you this question.

It's not the way. The virus wants to teach you. You are still developing. You think you can win in this way, but then another virus will come. And this one will mutate.

What you can do is stop it for a moment. We do not say that it's wrong. But it is not the solution of the problem. You will develop, and the virus will develop, and the next one will come. It is a cure for the moment. It can help and protect life. It's okay. But it is not the solution. You will not win. It will go forward. And it will get worse and worse. The whole life on Earth. People have to stop!

Ask something about yourself. You want to save the whole world. You want to, but you can't. It's not on you.

People have to learn. But they are blind, and they do not want to hear our words. They think they know it better than us. We are not developed. We are the Forgotten Ones.

See the stone in the sea. Its calmness. It rests in itself. Also in thunder, the rough sea, it still stands there, this rock. You can stand there like a rock. You have to stand there. Let the waves come and go. You will be stronger than the sea. The rock is stronger than the sea. You are not the rough sea. You have to let it come and go. And stand on your place and believe in yourself.

Believe in your strength. Your power. Your wisdom. Your love.

Keep staying where you are. But do not hide yourself in the forests. Ask yourself where this rock wants to stand. You only need to ask and find your place where you want to stay in these rough times. You can't flee out of these waves, but you can find your place to be strong. You will overcome these storms. You will. And we will help you with this from the Other Side of life.

Like the buffalo. It stands or walks in the storm and gets stronger.

Don't be afraid. Don't hide yourself. You're on your way.

Stand there and believe in yourself and your power and guides.

We lead you through this. It's not the first storm for you. Believe in yourself and your power that can overcome every storm. Trust in yourself.

Don't be afraid of these storms. You will need to learn through this. You have had your storms and they will have their storms. And we will meet sometime on the Other Side, to celebrate what you have done in this storm. And we need you for this on your side of life.

Feel the healing power. We send you the trust, power, self-confidence you need in this time.

We send you healing energy now. You can feel it. We heal your fears, your sorrows and your grief. Trust in yourself and be free.

Report of a Participant about the Past Circles

„I have been with Diana in her development circle for 5 years. I could feel the increase in energy in this circle. It got more intense from year to year. Although we sit together in this medium circle, I also felt a constant development of my senses. Little by little I became calmer, was able to perceive and feel more and more things and experienced an ever-growing peace within me but also outside and around me.

Now I was full of expectation what would happen in the trance circle. There we were told not to do anything but concentrate on the medium, send energy and strength to support Diana in her spiritual development.

Already at the first session I felt a difference to the development circle. The energy was different, it was more focused, and the room was full. Full of what I did not know. But I could feel the change. We were focused on Diana, and soon I saw her aura strengthen. It shone brighter and ran like a waterfall along her hair and arms. When Diana started to speak, the aura intensified again and shone brighter. There was a very peaceful atmosphere in the room.

When Diana started to speak, her face changed and other faces appeared one after the other, which quickly changed and also came back. This increased from session to session. The faces changed, other new ones were added, and those already seen reappeared. From time to time her aura grew stronger and brighter. A bright light flowed along her outer body, but also around her face and down from her throat chakra. The arms lit up partially. This light came and went. The colors of the aura also intensified. She was white in the first few sessions. The colors changed from green, magenta to a strong magenta that mixed with purple tones. This was particularly evident on November 18, 2020.

I am writing this on November 25th, 2020, and I am keen to see how it will continue. What I am writing here now are all experiences until November 18, 2020. What is very remarkable is that a fog forms around Diana as soon as she starts to speak. Her appearance steps back. It is enveloped in a colored veil that is getting stronger and more opaque. I could see that when the contact with her spirit guides was stronger then this fog was also stronger.

Her language changed. Sometimes the words were soft and delicate, and then again decisive and powerful. Depending on which spirit guide was in charge. The faces changed, and from time to time I could see that they were faces that had been there from the first time. But I could also recognize new ones.

A face was very present every time. It's a male face that has little or no hair. The face is round to elongate and wears round, rimless glasses. It reminds me of the face of Edgar Cayce.

Another face reminded me of an Indian, with dark skin. Another one looked like a Chinese and had a small pointy goatee. A woman was there, too. She looked humble and wise, an older woman. Another face that appeared every time was very impressive. It had a high hairline. The hair was curly. The face is narrower at the top and wider at the bottom, and the chin is also framed by a curly beard. He looked like an ancient scholar, like a philosopher. Diana later showed me a picture of Andrew Jackson Davis and I was almost shocked because he strongly reminded me of this "professor" I thought I saw. The times when Diana spoke became longer and longer, initially it was only a quarter of an hour twice, but on November 18th, 2020 it was already almost a full hour. The aura changed, becoming brighter and stronger sometimes. But this veil was visible almost throughout. We were also allowed to ask questions. I was surprised at the answers, which also gave concrete clues to personal questions. Honest answers that didn't embellish anything and were exactly right.

Now I would like to report how I feel personally at these meetings. I feel the energies very strongly every time.
Already in advance, that is hours in advance, I can feel that often the health problems I have are worsening.

Twice they were so strong that I thought I couldn't take part in the circle. This intensification of symptoms also sometimes occurs during the circle. Once I felt hands touching me and stroking my spine. I also had the feeling that my cervical vertebrae were being adjusted. These aggravations subsided after the circuit, sometimes this lasts up to 24 hours. After that I feel a relief of my problems every time. Basically, I have the feeling that it works with me."

U. D.

The Circle of Life

Trance Speaking November 25, 2020

We are the Forgotten Ones. We are here from the Other Side of life. We thank you for being here, for connecting with our world and believing in our world and in us.

We are here with a message for you. For your time and planet. For your soul.

We are here, and we thank you for being here with us.

Believe in yourself, in your way.

Be like an eagle in the wind. Flying in the highest winds, that's possible. Not to stay on the ground. To see the higher picture. More from this world than from the ground.

We are here and believe in our vision. In our clan. In our connection with Mother Earth.

Feel the energy of Mother Earth underneath your feet. Feel the power of this Earth. Connect with this power and believe in yourself.

We are here to connect you with this power to go through the storms of life. Through the chaos and the fears.

People have missed the right direction. They have missed the right pathway, the right junction.

They did not see the truth. They were only interested in themselves, not in this Earth. In this planet and the whole and in society.

We are here to remind you of this. To see the bigger picture of your world.

Fly like the eagle with us. Don't stay at your tree.

We send you healing power into your heart, energy of life from Mother Earth. Feel it in your heart and your feet and your body. We send you the healing power now. Feel the healing power. Now.

We sent you trust. Self-confidence and love.

See yourself like a tree in the wind. Only the strongest ones can stand it, because of their roots. You need deep roots to Mother Earth. Her power, her trust, her life energy.

People forget to live in peace with Mother Earth. They don't live in their life force. They destroy it.

They destroy this planet, with their thoughts, greed.

We send you the power of Mother Earth.

Feel it in your heart. The strength, the power and the love.

Be like the puma who can run fast and doesn't lose the right sight. You forgot the whole picture of life.

People are not interested in it. They are only looking for the best for themselves, not for the whole, for this Earth, the animals. For the life on this planet and other people.

Be like the butterfly which goes through dark times to grow and to transform itself. To make the best of itself. People go through this transformation at this time. They think it's dark, and they do not like it. They don't want to be in this process. They want to be the butterfly, but they have to go into the silence in the dark, to get evolved.

The times are here to make the best out of yourself.

But mankind has the choice. Many people do not choose the good way of life.

You can ask questions if you want.

Question: Can you tell us something about how we can solve our energy problem on Earth? Which forms of energy should we use or discover?

Answer: Mankind is blind for these other energies. They do not want them. They do not try them. They are blind. They think they have to destroy energy to get energy. They don't understand the word energy.

They think they have to destroy these „Earth Things" to use energy, but that's wrong. They have to find a way, to do it better. People are blind. We try to inspire them. We help and find new ways to protect this Earth, but they are blind. They find new ways for old energies and destroy Mother Earth.

It's not the point to find new energy. It's the point to live in the energy you have found in the balance. Not to destroy so much of it. Not to use so much energy. For this life.

The virus wants you to stop. To go a step back. Give yourself a break, Mother Earth a break. Don't use so much energy in your life.

It's not about new ways. It's about a new way of living in harmony with this world.

People take everything for granted and want more and more. But there is not enough there for their wishes and plans.

It's the same with other kinds of energy. They will destroy this Earth, maybe more than you can believe. More than you can imagine. Maybe it's a blessing that they do not have more energy to destroy this world. Think about this.

Things are not so easy to solve as you think.

The heart is the problem. The way of life of humans.

Mankind has to change.

People do not want to give things up. They want more and more and their lives back.

They have not learnt from this. So there will come the next lesson to learn.

Question: What kind of drive should our cars have? What should we drive them with? With which form of energy?

Answer: It is not on me to answer this. The answer is in the answer to your last question. It's time to give this Earth a break. Even if you have new energies the cars will destroy this Earth. There are too many of them. Think of the elements you need to produce the cars. The streets for which the forests have to disappear.

It's not only the energy which you need for your cars. The cars are the problem. Your whole industry is a problem. Mankind is destroying our Earth.

We lived in peace and harmony with this Earth. We only took what we needed to live. But these times are gone.

I don't know if mankind will find other energies. Which ones? The problem is not solved.

Question: From where do you speak to us? Are you in a certain dimension? Or are you close to us? Where are you?
Answer: We are in another dimension. But only one step away from your world.

We live in a higher vibration than yours. Here is more light, wisdom, knowing.

We see your world like the eagle from a higher position. And that causes us pain.

When we see how mankind lives, feels, treats each other, animals and this life on Earth. Many people live in a dark cloud. A dark world, full of dark emotions, thoughts, behavior.

We are on the Other Side of this life. In the World of the Spirits, but we can't do anything from here. This is painful.

But we try it, try to inspire you. We hope that you can help to make this world a better place. We are here with you for this.

We lived in peace, and we took this peace with us into our world here, full of peace.

You will also take it with you when you go, and your world will be the same.

It's not on us on our side of life to change it. It's on you, where you are now. To change your life, your environment, your heart, your soul. Then you can take this with you into our world. And then we can meet in this light.

And you have to evolve. Yourself, your life.

Question: Can you tell us something about Atlantis? Does this continent still exist on Earth or is it covered by water and the ocean?

Answer: Why do you want to know it? Why do you ask for this?

These times are gone. It's destroyed. It's under the sea. Not there any longer. Why are people wondering about these old times? Why do they not look at their own world so that something like this doesn't happen again?

Atlantis did exist, but it's gone. People did not learn to live in harmony with this world. It happens again and again. Do not look back in time. Look towards the future, to the world existing now. Look at your own life. What can you change now so that it gets a better world?

Don't explore old nations. Explore your own life, this nation. Find out what's to do, that it will not happen to your life, to your world.

People destroyed this world so often. It's like a tree in the circle of its life. It's dying and growing, an evolution, a circle of life. Don't look back. Don't make the same mistakes.

Don't think that you can change the world as you want. Believe in the wisdom of this world, of nature, Mother Earth. Mother Earth is stronger. The elements are stronger than you. Mother Earth can destroy everything on this Earth through the elements.

It's a growth. A circle. This world needs healing. Clearing. You can do it or Mother Earth will do it, the elements. So better help this Earth to heal.

We send you light now, healing light for all of your bodies. The emotional, the mental, spiritual and physical body.

It has to be in harmony. Feel the light and the healing now. Feel the trust in yourself in your heart. And the trust in life in your feet. And the trust in God and the better life in your head. And the trust and the power of humans in your hands.

Feel all this, how it is connected. Feel the power inside you and outside of you and in this world. Believe that you can change this world to a better place.

People have to change. Their thoughts, their behavior. Their energy and the vibration.

Feel the power in all parts of your life, in your body and your soul and in your heart. We are here to help you through this. To make this world a better world, where people treat each other like friends, where no one is better than the other one. And no one wants to be the best, better than everyone else. Richer than everyone.

People have to find back to brotherhood and humanity and love.

You put this world out of balance. You see it in the weather, you see it in the elements, in nature. It's starving, burning. And the elements in yourself are out of control too. People do not live in harmony. They are full of anger, jealousy, hate. This energy is omnipresent on this Earth. Like dark clouds of your thoughts. Think about this.

It's about your world, your energy. It's not about where Atlantis was. It's about the behavior of mankind. It's a technical evolution, but not in your hearts and souls. The virus shows us that everyone is the same, that everyone needs to breathe the same air. No money helps to be safe. And it shows that people have to stay together, to help each other. To be as one.
Mankind has to grow together, but they separate more and more. They did not learn. They separate more and more.
We are here from the Other Side of life. We hope to help you through the storms of these times. To grow together, to send healing and trust.
The life on this Earth must change, or the Earth will change the life on this Earth.
Feel the energy of healing now.

Do you remember what I told you about the body and the stars and the energy when something is missing?

It's like your whole Earth. It's out of balance. So many energies are missing. Forests, animals, nature.

You removed it. You removed the life energy. The balance is out of control.

We always gave the Earth something back when we took something from her. But your generation is only taking, and all you give back does not live, it's death energy.

You remove the old forests. You destroy the spirits of nature. You destroy the world in which you are living.

People are blind for this. They don't think they need it. They only want to get their old lives back. But you cannot get all life back. Many things are destroyed forever.

You always do not want anything to change, but life is changing, it's a cycle of life.

You do not want to grow old. You do not want to lose anything. You want that everything stays the same, but that's not life.

Look again at the tree. It blossoms. It loses its life in winter. You could think it only loses its leaves, but it's getting a new life.

That's like you. You have to let things go. Go inside of you and go back in life like the bear, which goes to sleep in the winter and wakes to life again in the spring.

Nature lives in this cycle. Nature knows that life comes and goes, things come and go. You have to let go of things to get new things, your energy is a cycle of life. But people do not want to change. They want that everything stays the same. They do not want to lose anything, give anything up.

It must be more and more. But that's not the way in nature. You have to let things go for a new life. People could see that potential in the virus, this circle of life of nature. To let things go, go in silence. Let this be like a sleep in the winter, and then wake up to a new life, to a better life, with more energy. But people do not want to have this sleep. They do not want to let go. They want to have the old energies back, but that's not how this life goes. Everything is a circle in this life. Let the old things go, do not think about the old things. Let it go. Be it Atlantis, Lemuria or the Middle Ages. Let the old stories go.

Get inside yourself, heal yourself and find new energy in yourself in this moment you exist. And then wake up to a better life, to a new life, to a new circle of life. Like the flower in the spring or the tree.

The first I know about this society is, people have no more power to blossom again. They are stuck in the old energy. Do not be stuck. Let old things go.

Let good things grow in the darkness, in the peace, in the silence. Believe in the power of life, and you will see what's growing from this. Like the rock, I told you about before. Stay at his place in silence and peace and let it grow.

Don't think too much, about your past life and things that are gone. Take a break and dream your life in a better way and believe in it. We will help you with this and remind you of this.

Don't ask about old things, ask about new things that will come. And dream it in reality.
Don't think about old thoughts and plans. Create new ones and a new life, not only for yourself.

We surround you with our life force, with our love and with healing energies.
Thank you for being here. For being our friends and connecting with us.
Believe in yourself and your dream and a better world. Dream this world into a better place.

Perceptions in the Circle Room

As I progressed in my trance control development, there were more and more knocking noises in my circle room, which were also heard by the participants. It first reminded me of the Fox Sisters' experience, and we wondered if we should react to it, as Steven Upton had recommended in a lecture. These phenomena might be a sign of physical mediumship and show that one has a potential for it. But I have a lot of respect for physical circles and never wanted to deal with them. And I don't want to sit in any cabinet to this day, because I don't think that fits into our time. So I will not answer with a knock.

While listening to the audio recordings, I suddenly got the inspiration that it sounded like drumbeats. Like my shamanic frame drum. Very, very even, rhythmical and the energy in the room also increased.

During my shamanic travel evenings in my practice, the participants sometimes see my Indian drumming with me. And hear two drums. I don't even notice it while I'm drumming, but I sometimes wonder where I get the strength to drum from.

Be What You Are

Trance Speaking December 2, 2020

We are the Forgotten Ones. We are here from the Other Side of life. We're here to teach you, to work with you, to heal you. We are here and thank you for being here in this light. These times are special. We are here to help you through these times. With courage, faith and love to go through these times.

We send you healing now from our side of life.

Feel it in your heart and your body, everywhere you need this light. We send you blue light from our side of life now.

For calmness, peace, relaxation you need in these times, to go inward to find this peace, calmness and stillness. Feel it now, the blue light. We are sending it to you now. Feel it and heal with it. And violet from the cosmic realms.

We heal your fears from ancient times. We give you self-confidence, courage and trust.

Feel it in your heart and your body and mind.

We now send you this energy. To heal and trust. To believe in the goodness in this world that still exists.

You often only see the bad things. Cruel people, bad people. But there is still hope. And we thank you for this.

Hope to make things better. Done before. People have to wake up to a new energy and life. But they still want their old lives back. But this will not happen in this lifetime.

Feel the trust in your heart and the energy of life and hope and grace. Feel it now.

We now send you green energy you need in these times. Feel it now. Orange for healing and creativity.

People do not understand the vibration of colors. They are blind for the energies behind.

Feel the energy of the colors when they touch you. When you meditate with them. The vibration at your organs. We will teach you this.

What if a color is missing in the rainbow? Or if organs are missing in your body? It's the same. Not complete.

Stand up for the things you believe, do not hide. Do not make yourself small and bad.

As we said before, the truth is not with the loudest people. Don't hide yourself, but fly. Why don't you fly?

We send you the wings and the winds to fly, but you have to fly for yourself. Trust and fly.

Be calm when it's needed. And loud when it's needed. Stand up for your truth. Don't hide yourself.

When you are an eagle, you behave like an eagle, not like a mouse or a crow.

You have to be what you are, not what the others are. Behave as you are. Don't make yourself small.

Be different. Don't try to be like the others are. Be the best version of what you are. Be yourself and trust yourself.

Go through the storms and believe in yourself. Don't hide in the forest.

Give yourself the opportunity to grow, to learn. But you have to start.

Do you want to ask something?

Question: Can I ask a personal question?
Answer: Yes.
Question: I am still looking for what I can really do as a life task for my life, for the Earth, for people. And I have the feeling that it is possible for me to lead deceased souls who are not yet in the light into the light. I do this with columns of light. Is this a task that I should do? Or is that no way for me? Would it be my job to take care of it?
Answer: Did you make the journey we asked you to make? Travel with your legs? Have you asked them, where they want to go? You have to find it for yourself.

But it's such an honour to have you here to help these souls to see the light. They have to go forward. The souls hold themselves, like you hold yourself in your forest, on your tree. You all have to go forward, and maybe you can help each other to grow. Help these people to the Other Side. You can do this. But this is not your whole life purpose. Look at yourself. What do you want to do? What are you here for? There is more than this.

You can help them, do it, but there is more. Ask yourself where you have to go, and then go. We ask you to fly where you want to go. They are not lost souls. They are protected, but they have to move. We need you for this. Help them to go to the light.

What do you want to ask?

Question: Will the Corona Virus go away on its own?
Answer: We can't answer this. It's not on us. It's on you. How people will behave and grow. The virus wants to teach mankind, but they have not learned it.

Maybe this virus will go away, but there will come another one. It's not important what the name of the virus is.

There will be viruses in this world, and you have to learn from this, that all is connected, that people have to work together and to protect each other. But many people do not want it, they still want their old lives back. But the virus will not disappear in this way. You have to learn this, to learn more than this. It's not about the virus. It's about the message of the virus.

Every pandemic goes its way and will end, also this one, also this virus, but then another one will come. Maybe next year, maybe in ten or one hundred years. It's on you to learn from this. To heal this world, not only from a virus.

Maybe you are like a virus for Mother Earth? She does not ask when you will go away.

What is needed is to live in harmony together. To learn to protect. Maybe Mother Earth feels like you, with the virus. Think about it.

We send you healing now, green energy. Fill your whole heart with it.

The virus is out of control. Everything is developing higher and higher, the viruses, the technology. It's not as it was. That's not possible, to go back in time. You have to stop it. Stand still and look behind, look back at what you have created.

The virus comes from nature, has developed in nature. You have to let nature live for itself. Mankind is playing God in nature and in the creation. You want to change all that you want to have, the animals, the forests, the food. All this is not natural anymore.

You think that this is growth, technology. Many people are proud of what they do, what they create. But there's no life in it. No harmony. They are playing God.

Nature and the virus show this like a mirror. Everything has developed, but not in a healthy way.

The virus is out of control and nature and Mother Earth, too. But mankind, people do not learn from this. They are creating new life, and that's what the virus will do.

How can you stop it? It's not on us.

People have to wake up before it's too late. You went through this again and again, but you have not learnt to live in harmony and peace. Don't play God.

Nature and Mother Earth will stop this play, if you do not stop it yourself.

What do children learn? Do they learn to live in harmony with nature? Do they learn something about nature? No.

They learn about technology. They learn about the human things, what humans are proud of on your side of history, but not the history of Mother Earth, what happens with Mother Earth.

It's always about mankind. Not about nature and Mother Earth.

Mother Earth is crying and wants to stop people, to have a break and not to destroy everything, also themselves.

You have destroyed the elements, the air, the water, the Earth. You can not produce this in your laboratories. It's not life force what you produce and you can't fill anything with this energy. When you have destroyed it, it will be gone.

You cannot create God's energy. You failed in this before. You tried to do it, but you can't.

You have destroyed all that is full of life in nature. The forest, the glaciers. Think about this.

Where do you get this life force? In your cities? In your houses? Or in nature? But mankind is destroying nature. This virus comes out of nature. It comes from the animals. Maybe from the forests to people.

It wants to stop people. But they are blind. They only want to have their old lives back, their lives that destroy this Earth! We are so sad about this.

Our Indian Nations told this to the white man. They don't hear. They don't want to hear what we say. They don't want to learn. They think they know it better.

Nature will get more aggressive to protect itself from this play and this development. But people only look at the virus and not what's behind it.

We now send you healing again. Energy from our side of life. Feel it in your whole body and heal by this.

Thank you for being what you are. And that your heart is beating for this Mother Earth. We need you for this and thank you for this.

Look after yourselves and do not forget yourselves and Mother Earth.

We send you healing light into your throat so that you can speak your truth. Do not hide anymore. Speak the truth. We need you for this.

Don't hide in the forest. The forest needs you here. Don't hide in the world of the dead souls. You can help them, but they are dead. Help this world, this nature, this Mother Earth. What still is alive, before it's too late and all is dead. We need you here. Ask your legs and your soul: Where's your place to speak this truth?

Be a speaker of this Earth. We need you for this, to protect this life force. Not for death.

Many people see death, but they are blind for life. They are not interested in this Earth and nature anymore.

Thank you.

The Weather is out of Control

Trance Speaking December 9, 2020

We are the Forgotten Ones. We are here to teach you our wisdom from the Other Side. We are here to help you through this time.

People do not recognize what's going on. They only see the moment. What's going on in their own lives but not in this world. They don't change anything for the better, for Mother Earth. They only want to change their lives back to normal, but this will not happen.

The virus will play with them next year. You think you have it under control, this world, this nature. The experiments. But that's not true. Nothing is under control without love.

Nature reacts on people. It's an evolution out of control. You destroy this Earth. The rainforest, animals, life. And you cry when something is destroyed in your own life, when you can't go back to your normality. But what is normal?

Life of mankind isn't normal. Is not true. It's not under control. Not in harmony with this Earth. To which normality do you want to go back? To your technical world? With the fun, egoism and ignorance?

We are here, because we have lived in an other world. Full of peace, harmony and empathy, but that's gone.

We are the Forgotten Ones because we lived in a world that is forgotten now, destroyed by the so-called civilization.

We send you healing light now for your heart to heal all grief, disappointment and fear.

We send you this green and blue light for this now. Fill your heart with it to heal yourself and this world.

Society gets cool, the climate hot. It's out of control. You change the weather. People suffer from it. But many are blind for this. They do not care.

Not only for Mother Earth, they don't care about each other. They left people behind, because they think they are not so developed as themselves.

People have a wrong picture of wealth. They're proud of things that only have a meaning for themselves and this society, not in this world, not for Mother Earth.

They are blind for nature, harmony. They are looking for other things they can buy and live for. But this destroys this Earth and their soul.

Everyone wants to be better. Everyone looks after himself. And everyone is blind for what's behind their lives.

Why are you here on this Earth? What's the great meaning behind this?

Why is the virus there?

Look at each other and help, to make the community grow together.

The virus is developing, changing. But not for your best, just like you.

We send you light to heal and trust.

Do you want to ask something?

Question: Is it possible for you to make diagnoses in our body?

Answer: We can do this. We can see into your soul, into your body, into your mind, into your whole existence. We see your fears, illnesses and what's behind.

You're all full of fears. Fear to be not good enough. Fear to be lost. Fear to get ill that gets you ill. And the fear of the fear.

We are here to explain you this with time.

Look into your heart. What are you hiding from? What are you afraid of? It's all in your heart.

What are you not living? What are you afraid of? What are you running away from?

All your illness comes from this. Not living your potential. Living in fear. Not trusting yourself. You need to trust yourself. But you do not trust your body.

How can you trust yourself if you think you are too weak, not strong enough. You're stronger than you think, your body is stronger than you think.

Believe in yourself and your body and go forward. And live your strength. Find your strength in yourself and not in other people's strength.

Develop your own strength and go your way and live your potential and do not hide in your forest.

Everything comes from fear. All your illness. The first fear was to live. This is the strongest one. You have to heal this. We can do this.

We send you healing light for this. Self-confidence. Trust in yourself. You all need this trust in yourself. Believe in yourself. Do not listen to what others think of you. Think for yourself.

What do you want to think about yourself? Don't think what others think about you.

You know this, but you do not live this. Believe in yourself, and then all can heal in your heart and soul.

Do you want to ask something about Mother Earth?

Question: Can we do anything concrete for the Earth? Can we influence anything with the currents in the sea? For example the Gulf Stream in the Atlantic. Are there opportunities for people to make it stay that way and not to weaken?
Is it in the power of men to achieve something there?

Answer: It's too late to change this now. The weather reacts on the humans. All humans have to change.

At those times there was the possibility to change something. To heal the climate. To stand still for a moment. But people missed this opportunity. They missed to heal this world.

The weather is out of control. It's hard to stop it. It's possible, but it's very late for this.

Maybe the virus will stop people. Mother Earth wants to stop people, make them stand still. But mankind won't stand still, they won't change their way of life. So the weather will develop in this way, too.

Mankind changed this Earth, this weather. The whole life on this planet. What can we do?

We can cry, we can pray. Or we can ask people to change. We are here to ask people to change. To bring our message in this world. We need you for this. You on your own can't do anything, only mankind together can. But they are doing other things in hate. They do not trust us anymore. They think they know it better. They want to know it better. Everyone wants to know it best. They don't want to ask us.

They don't want to listen to us or to Mother Earth. They are looking at their stars and have forgotten Mother Earth.

And everything is a reaction to this.

We are here to help you through this, to help you to understand.

There's so much more behind. We try to teach it to you. But you have to find a new picture of the whole, of the Earth.

See this Earth as a living thing. With consciousness, with emotions. What can you see when you think like that about Mother Earth?

She is full of negative emotions of this society, of this mankind. Like a dark aura of energies around. You need to clean it, you need to heal it.

Life on this Earth has to stand still for a while. We have had this before, and it will come again... Maybe with your free will or maybe it will happen when Mother Earth does it as she likes.

This Earth has to stand still like the jet streams stand still. It's a mirror of your society. That people don't want to stand still. They want to have their old lives back. But this will not heal your weather, this will not heal Mother Earth, and this will not change anything to a positive direction. Everything will get all the more worse than before. Life on this Earth has to stand still to heal and to regenerate.

Many people stay on their tree, but this is not what we think they should do. They hide themselves. They are shy. They are quiet, they don't say anything. But this will not change anything or help this Earth. You have to take your right position and help this Earth before it's too late.

Did you ask your legs? No, you didn't. But you should do so! You all have to find your place. And trust in yourself and your power.

But you on your own can't stop or change what's going on. But you can be a part of the solution. We are here for this. Think about this.

Feel the energy of Mother Earth underneath your feet. Connect with Mother Earth and her power. Feel her heartbeat, her life. People have forgotten to feel the life of Mother Earth. They don't see it. But they also don't feel it. All that is natural in your world. You have forgotten to feel Mother Earth underneath your feet, when you go into the forest, to the beach. Not only to see all things, to feel them. Be with your soul. Feel it. People in my world at our time helped Mother Earth. We talked to her. We felt when she was not happy with us. We were thankful for all that she gave us. All food. The water. We thanked, and we gave something back. People forget to give something back, to thank, to be thankful.

Question: Can I ask another question?
Answer: Yes.
Question: Are there also influences from outside the Earth, from the cosmos, which influence our climate here? Or is it caused exclusively by humans or are these also cosmic influences from outside?
Answer: Everything is connected in our universe. But more than what comes from outside is what our Earth brings into the universe. Not the universe is the problem, the Earth is the problem.

The Earth is not in harmony and this goes outside into the universe, and other planets react. And then they react to the Earth and you again. It's a mirror.

Of course there is influence from other planets. But that's not the problem, the problem is on this Earth. Do you remember what I told you weeks before? What if one planet is missing? The whole energy of this cosmic world is out of control. But what if the energy of one planet is not full of harmony? If the potential is gone?

What if your body has an organ that is not healthy, that's ill? It influences the whole body. And this is what's in your cosmos reality. The Earth is ill, and the planets are reacting. There won't be any more harmony in this cosmic world if we do not change this Earth back to harmony. So maybe, the cosmic answer will come. Maybe they want to change something. To bring it back to harmony, to stop what's going on. Think about this.

On Earth mankind looks for the reason of all outside of themselves. But they have to look inside and change things themselves. Everyone has to change and the whole world, too. It's the same with this Earth. Think about it and help to bring a change into this whole universe, before it's too late.

Everything is connected, but this planet has been changed by mankind. Look outside of this world into the universe. People take their rubbish there. It's not enough to put everything into the water, into the Earth. Everywhere you can see the footsteps of mankind. But not good ones.

Many things can't be changed in your lifetime. It is too late for many mistakes in this world to change. Seeds have been planted, and some seeds can't be destroyed by you. You can only watch what is growing out of these plants. And they have to ask their grandchildren for forgiveness for what they have done. They have to forgive many things, but they are blind. That's how it will go forward. People have to change before it's too late.

We are here to help you through this change, and we'll ask you to go into a better direction, if we see what's happening now. It is not on us. We can't do anything from our side of life. It's on mankind that are living. But they have to open their minds, their consciousness and especially their hearts for this Earth and all that is living on it.

They have to protect, not only themselves. They have to protect the whole life on this Earth before it's too late. Before this life is going away.

They will know what they will miss when it's too late. Mankind often misses things when they've lost them, but then it's too late. They have to wake up before it's too late. For the beauty of this life and for all on Mother Earth.

They have time for this, but it's passing quickly. We pray that they wake up for a better world and peace and harmony and love. We want to help to create this world on your side of life.

We thank you for being here. Believe in yourself and the goodness in this world. And visualize a better world in peace and harmony and love for what's living. We hope for this on our side of life.

Live Your Vision

Trance Speaking December 16, 2020

We are the Forgotten Ones, we are here from the Other Side of life. We thank you for being here with us. These times are special. We are here to talk about this. People still don't want to change. They want their old lives back. Their history is not full of good things. You can't be proud of everything. It's not good to go back in history, to repeat it, your history. You have to go forward, but not in the way like people think. They only think about technical development and they don't develop their soul. They don't develop their heart. They only develop dead things. But that's not good. The material develops without mankind. They have changed things, they have changed Mother Earth, but they don't want to change their lives. But you could and you should do it now.

You have changed everything that's on this Earth.
Nature, the elements, the water, the air. Not much is left that you did not change. Only things you did not know or did not find. Like the arctic. It's not safe anymore. Mankind wants to have all, but that's not good.

How can you change things in a better way?

Look for the big picture. Grace. Love. Empathy. Brotherhood.

Change it for the whole and not for your own.

No one is better than the other one. Although they think they are.

They have their politics and their beliefs and destroy this Earth.

Animals are disappearing, but not only them. Energy is going away. The harmony is going away. Things are going away, forever.

They have to put an end to what they're doing. This world has to grow together now. The virus could help, but they fail. So the next thing will happen soon.

What can you do?

Be in your heart. Live with your heart. Don't think things over. Feel it in your heart, if it's good. If it's full of love and kindness, that's all.

We lived in a world together in harmony. No one was better than the other one. No one wanted to be better when we lived in harmony. Then the white man came. And the harmony was gone. They wanted us to be like them. And some tried to do it. But this was the end of all, this way of life. We were not allowed to live our way of life. These times are gone, and we know they will never come back as they were.

But you can learn from this. To treat each living thing in another way. To be thankful and kind. Change your behavior, and this world will change, too.

We send you energy to heal. To go into the calmness and harmony, into balance. Feel it now. We now send you green energy to heal. Feel it now.

Ask your children how they want to live when they are small. When they are still in their heart and soul. You can learn from them.
But people change them and their way of living. They don't see the potential in each child.
Why are they here? What's their life purpose?
To live your life, to be like you?
Maybe they are here to change something.
Ask them what they want to be in their hearts. Listen!

We send you healing light into your heart.
That you go back in time, to your inner child and ask your child, yourself: What is your purpose? Why are you here? What do you want to change, what do you want to do? You will remember. Then listen to yourself. Your inner child. Go inside and ask yourself: What's your vision?
You have to do it now.
What are you burning for? What do you want to do? What do you want to change for this Earth?
Go your own way! The way no one went before.

You can find it in your heart. Why are you here? And then do this. And find and live your vision. We help you with this. And we send you still energies to follow your heart and way. Feel it in your heart, this energy of trust, belief, hope and love. Thank you for this.

Do you want to ask something?

Question: Is there any herbal remedy that can be used to cure the Corona Virus? Is there a possibility? About herbs, herbal medicine?
Answer: We are not here to do this. It's not allowed in your technical world.

We have this energy. The flowers, the crops, but in this time they are not there for you. You have to heal it in another way.

You have to heal society. But that's not possible with a herb, a flower, something from nature.

You are destroying nature. The herbs that could help are disappearing. Maybe there's something that can help, but it's on you to change this world.

This virus comes from nature, but it is not treated with nature. And it's not on us to say something, to help.

You have to change. Go inside and find it for yourself. Mankind has to find the solution. We are not allowed to help you with this.

Don't be afraid. Go inside and find the possibilities.

You have homeopathy, herbs, things for your immune system. It's not new, it's there. But it's not about this. You have to change and heal the immune system of this planet not only of yourself. You are only looking for healing. Herbs for yourself, but Mother Earth needs it. The animals, nature. It's not in harmony like yourself.

You have destroyed nature. The living space of the animals. You have to heal this first, and then the virus can go away.

What was society like during the Spanish Flu? How did people live? What was society like? What has changed in this time? Look at this. The parallels to today. Look at this.

We send you healing now. Feel it in your whole body and in your heart.

Why does the virus get aggressive and different? Why does it mutate?

It's playing with you. There is not one herb to treat it. It's more difficult, because it will change. It's playing with you. You have to study it. Talk to it and find the truth behind it. It's a living thing.

Why are you here and why is the virus here? What can you learn from this?

Look at the signature of the virus. One virus can do nothing. It's the mass. There are uncountable viruses in this world. Too many to know, too many to count, too many to find, too many to treat, too many to remove. Maybe as many as mankind.

One virus can't do anything. The whole of all, that is the answer. One person can't treat, remove this virus. Only the whole. The whole world has to stand together, to treat this disease. It's not about one herb. It's about the meaning behind. People have to hold together as we told you before. You have to grow together. You have to connect. The whole world has to grow together. Help each other. But people are separated, they look in different directions, they fight against each other.

Your society is not like this virus that works together. You're spread, disconnected and not in harmony.

Everyone wants to go his way. Everyone wants it better. There's no consciousness together. It's a chaos. And the virus will help to show it to you. This chaos in your society is out of control. What can we do?

Mankind has to grow together with harmony and help each other. And go forward as a union for a bigger vision, for a bigger purpose, for the whole.

Think about it, this separation and the union and what has failed. Think about this until we meet again.

Go inside the following times. Meditate. Talk to your legs. Ask yourself where you want to fly from your tree. Not only for your own vision. For the whole, for the society, for this world, for Mother Earth. Where can you help the big picture, the bigger vision of this world, to come together in peace, brotherhood, humanity and freedom?

How can you help that people grow together?

There is so much to heal in this world. How can you start?

You will feel like a little bird in your tree, not able to do something. Feeling little and weak. But you're weak on your own. You have to find other birds, other people to build this bigger vision. There are souls like you that you have to find. One bird in its little tree cannot change this world, just like a virus on its own.

You have to grow together in love, humanity and kindness. Trust yourself and the good in each person that exists. And it needs to be developed and to be lived. Not for yourself, for the whole. We hope to help you with this. Like our clan, like the stars. As I told you before, do you remember? One organ cannot do all on its own.

What if one organ is missing? What if you are missing in the whole picture?

You have your place in this world for freedom, harmony, love and healing.

You have to find your place. Like the star in the sky has its place.

What if you are missing on your place?

Don't feel like the little bird in its tree. Start to fly to your place to help this world to grow together and make it better for the next generations to come.

Fly. Even if you don't know where you will be landing and flying to. And trust yourself and your wings. They will get stronger when you fly. But you have to fly for your own.

You have to fly and find your place in this world. We hope for this and thank you for this.

Report of a Participant about the Past Circles

In the meantime the connection between the medium and its spirit guides is going faster and stronger. We have only sat in silence for a few minutes when Diana begins to speak. The greeting is now very familiar.

Although my English is not very good, I was able to understand so much that every week the messages continued from where they had ended a week before.

That evening of November 16th 2020 I noticed that the aura, which grew stronger from week to week, changed particularly quickly and intensely. It got very wide. At first it was bright, but quickly the colors changed. An intense turquoise shone around Diana. It was particularly strong upwards, but the aura also expanded on the sides. Then I saw a strong glow that flickered and moved. It started at the head and continued downwards. And it was a very intense color, an ultramarine as I know it from my paintings and from the pure pigments. Only they shine so intensely. It looked beautiful. This colored glow enveloped the medium in such a way that it could only be seen in the background. I felt that the chakras were glowing.

The color was not rigid either, but enveloped the medium like a veil of mist. It was very moving and impressive.

In retrospect, after learning the content of the message, I found that it was a very important, deep and touching message.

Now I had the feeling that the Forgotten Ones wanted to emphasize the importance of the message with these intense colors. It was a very touching experience. I am grateful that I was able to experience this.

During the sessions it happened to me that my knee problems got very bad. Sometimes I found it difficult to remain sitting in silence.

Now while I am writing this from my memory, five weeks have passed since the last circle on December 16, 2020, and my knee problems are noticeably improving. I am very grateful to the Forgotten Ones and the medium for that.

I always find the circle to be very powerful and constructive, and I am grateful that I can be there and experience it all. It really is an experience. If you read this, it could be that you doubt the words. But when you've experienced it, you don't doubt. Then you don't believe any of this either, you know it. And I don't want to miss this experience anymore. It enlarges me. This can no longer be taken from me either. Because one thing is certain. You cannot "de-know", lose what you know.

I am already looking forward to further encounters with the "Forgotten Ones". In the meantime we are really familiar with them, and they impress us with their modest, but determined manner. Sometimes they seem a little sad, but they are thankful for being allowed to join us."
U. D.

Epilogue

The Home Circle this book is about began on September 16, 2020 and ended on December 16, 2020.

I'm sure the Forgotten Ones still have a lot to tell us, not just about the current pandemic. But since it is no longer possible to hold meetings for the time being due to the tightened lockdown, I will now give their first messages to the world, especially since these words are so important at the moment.

Even if we hope to be able to return to a "normal life" soon, we should continue to take more care of each other in the future, as is necessary in this pandemic. It is not only important to pay attention to our fellow human beings, wearing masks in compliance with hygiene and distance rules, but also to Mother Earth and everything that lives on her. So that a positive future may grow from what we experienced last year. May people not simply return to their normality, but rather create a better world together, full of compassion, solidarity, tolerance and gratitude for Mother Earth.

Much of what mankind consciously or unconsciously destroys on this precious Earth can no longer simply be brought back.

Let's make sure that together we preserve what is still there. And maybe the virus just wants to force people to calm down a little more, so that they can focus on themselves, see this world with different eyes and recognize what is really important in life. Solidarity with one another and a growing together of all humanity. And let us consciously and gratefully give Mother Earth this break to heal.

We all travel on a road no one took before. Make this road a good one. Full of compassion, empathy, solidarity, tolerance and love.

Over the past months in 2020, my spirit guides have repeatedly spoken through me about the spiritual background of the Covid-19 pandemic or the destruction of the environment and the reaction of Mother Earth to us humans.

During the time of this pandemic I was also sitting regularly twice a week with a participant from my training in trance. This participant lives in San Francisco and was hit by the devastating forest fires in California in the summer of 2020. It was raining ash, the sky looked like the apocalypse, and people were not able to breathe. They had to wear masks not only because of the virus, but also because of the ash rain. During this time I spoke to her in a trance.

My guides said through me that all this was about breathing and air. Not only the Covid-19 pandemic is about breathing and suffocation.

It's the same with the forest fires in the USA. Or what the Black Lives Matter movement is based on ... The feeling of not being able to breathe.

My Indian guide said that people would be grateful to see the sun again after the US forest fires. When the air is clear again. Everything has become too natural for people. Also the air. May they pray, thank the Earth.

It's about air, being able to breathe, not only with Covid-19 infections. These fires and the virus affect everyone. Humans cannot breathe, they cannot get fresh air. They are not independent as they think. Everything is connected. Now it affects everyone. Regardless of nationality and skin color. Regardless of the possessions and money.

My Indian told her the sun would come again and painted a sun with my left hand at the same time.

The corona virus is round like a circle, a unit with no beginning – no end. See it as a symbol.

The individual should find back to this unit. Every person should find back to this unit, the wholeness. Into love.

See this world as a unit. Mother Earth. People are at their own. Many are alone. But find to a new wholeness and take care of each other.

Looking for the big picture, for the well-being of all. For Mother Earth. For all creatures, and finally for all humans.

Trance Speaking August 20, 2020 for Kahuna K./Hawaii

Kahuna K. lost the battle of cancer but not the battle of the soul. Her soul.

She brought down the energy of the stars and connected it to the energy of the earth. The Kilauea volcano is full of power. Life energy. Joy. That embodied her.

She looks at us from the stars. And helps us to find our soul star. The soul who guides us in these dark times. Which shows the way. To look inward. To find the light. In ourselves and to go on. She helps us with this. She is a star that shines on our way. We just have to see this star and move on. She helps us with that. From the stars. And helps us to be lighthouses. For other people in this Corona time. We should form an even larger network of light. We need a larger one. To help each other. To go forward. Out of the dark. From fear and anger into love. The stars are with you and around you. The stars send life. Read the energy of the stars. The stars bring light to the darkest moments, and illluminate.

There is a deep transformation of mankind, and it is the darkest moment of the soul. The stars shine for you. Follow your soul. Humans should go within. You are not alone.

You came from the stars. Believe in yourself. Help others find the light inside themselves. Let your light shine. Kahuna K. transformed herself to the betterment of human kind. And that's what we can do... together.

Zeitfracht Medien GmbH
Ferdinand-Jühlke-Straße 7
99095 Erfurt, Deutschland
produktsicherheit@kolibri360.de